Paul Revere
and the Bell Ringers

By Jonah Winter
Illustrated by Bert Dodson

Aladdin

New York London Toronto Sydney Singapore

To Ed Denmead —J. W.
To Kody —B. D.

First Aladdin edition November 2003

Text copyright © 2003 by Jonah Winter
Illustrations copyright © 2003 by Bert Dodson

ALADDIN PAPERBACKS
An imprint of Simon & Schuster Children's Publishing Division
1230 Avenue of the Americas, New York, NY 10020

Book design by Lisa Vega
The text of this book was set in Century Old Style.

Printed in the United States of America
2 4 6 8 10 9 7 5 3 1

Library of Congress Cataloging-in-Publication Data
Winter, Jonah.
Paul Revere and the bell ringers / by Jonah Winter ; illustrated by
Bert Dodson.
p. cm. — (Ready-to-read. Level 2)
Summary: Young Paul Revere and his friends form a club whose members ring
the bells at Christ Church, an experience which teaches him responsibility and
other lessons that he uses as an adult in the American Revolution.
ISBN 0-689-85636-9 (library ed.) — ISBN 0-689-85635-0 (pbk.)
1. Revere, Paul, 1735–1818—Juvenile literature. 2. Revere, Paul, 1735–1818—Childhood
and youth—Juvenile literature. 3. Change ringing—Massachusetts—Boston—History—
18th century—Juvenile literature. 4. Statesmen—Massachusetts—Biography—Juvenile
literature. 5. Massachusetts—Biography—Juvenile literature.
[1. Revere, Paul, 1735–1818—Childhood and youth. 2. Clubs. 3. United States—History—
Revolution, 1775–1783—Biography.] I. Dodson, Bert, ill. II. Title. III. Series.
F69.R43.W46 2003
973.3'311'092—dc21

2002008610

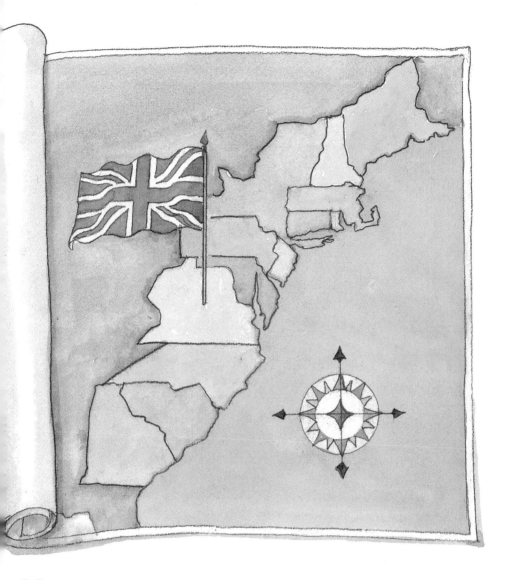

Many years ago,

before America was a country,

it was called the thirteen colonies,

and it was under British rule.

Way up north in a colony
called Massachusetts,
there was a town by the sea.
It had narrow streets
that were crowded with people.
This town was called Boston.

Tucked away

on one very crooked street,

in one very dark house,

there lived a boy named Paul Revere.

Paul worked in his father's shop,
learning how to make things
with gold and silver.
While rich boys sat in school reading,
Paul melted and hammered metal
over a burning fire.

He sweat and strained

making teapots

and serving trays.

While he was hammering,
Paul heard his father
talking to customers
about many things.

They talked about Great Britain,
the country across the sea
that ruled the colonies.
There was another thing
that Paul *loved* to hear about:
clubs!

Grown-ups in Boston
loved clubs and meetings.
They also loved things called
rules and elections.
That's mostly what they talked about.
They gave Paul some ideas. . . .

One Sunday as Paul and his friends were walking through the narrow streets of Boston, they started talking about forming their own club.

"Why should our parents

have all the fun?"

Paul asked his friends.

"Right!" said Paul's friend John.

"But what kind of club should we form?"

While walking down a dirty street,
Paul and his friends
looked around
for the answer.

"I know," said Paul's friend Barth,

"let's start a street-cleaning club!"

"Hmmm," said Paul.

"Hmmm," said the other boys.

They kept on walking.

Seagulls squawked.

"I know," said Paul's friend Joseph,
"let's start a bird-watcher's club!"
"Hmmm," said Paul.
"Hmmm," said the other boys.

They kept on walking.
When they turned the corner,
they saw Christ Church,
the tallest building in Boston.
The church bells were ringing.

"I know," said Paul,

"let's form a bell ringing club."

The boys looked up at the bells,
ringing and ringing.

They were the most famous bells
in Boston.

You could hear them for miles!

"The question is," said Joseph,
"how do we get the church
to let us ring
the best bells in Boston?"

"Easy," said Paul.

"We write up a contract.
The contract will have the rules
of our club.
Then we sign the contract."
The boys went to Barth's house
to think about the contract.

Once a week in the evening,
the boys would ring the bells.
They would also have meetings
to vote on new rules.

The boys would ring the bells whenever the church wanted them to. If they forgot to show up, the boys would pay money to the church.

That is what the boys wrote

in their contract.

Paul and his friends signed the contract,

went to the church,

and talked to the priest.

He let them ring the bells!

Once a week the boys
visited the church,
where they learned bell ringing
from an older bell ringer.

There were eight bells in all.

Some were big,

and some were really big.

Each boy rang a bell or two,

and each bell made a different sound.

The boys learned how

to play songs on these bells.

It was fun!

But it was more than just fun.

In the bell ringing club,

the boys made their own rules.

No one told them what to do.

They were in charge.

That felt good.

It also felt good

to make a promise and keep it.

It felt good to make music

that the whole town could hear.

These things were still
important to Paul
when he became a man.
He joined clubs
that helped the colonies become
a separate country
with its own laws.

From the bell ringing club
Paul had learned about
helping his town.
These lessons gave Paul Revere
ideas about how to become
one of America's greatest patriots.

Here is a timeline of Paul Revere's life:

1734	Paul Revere is born in Boston's North End
1747	Paul Revere leaves school at thirteen years old to work in his father's gold and silversmith shop
1749	Paul Revere forms a bell ringing club with his friends
1754	Paul Revere's father dies; Paul takes over his father's business
1765	Paul is one of the earliest members of the Sons of Liberty, a club that fights against Great Britain
1773	The Sons of Liberty stage an important historical event called the Boston Tea Party; not really a party, it was a protest against Great Britain
1775	Paul makes his famous "midnight ride," to Lexington, Massachusetts, to alert Samuel Adams and John Hancock and nearby towns of the British invasion; the next morning the American Revolution begins
1776	The Declaration of Independence is created and signed; in this document the colonies declare their freedom from Great Britain, and for the first time are called the United States of America
1783	The American Revolution ends with the signing of the Treaty of Paris
1792	Paul Revere's company starts making church bells
1818	Paul Revere dies at the age of eighty-three